SEVEN LAST WORDS
& EIGHT WORDS
OF EASTER

SEVEN LAST WORDS & EIGHT WORDS OF EASTER

Meditations for
Your Journey to Pentecost

MARY SHARON MOORE

AWAKENING VOCATIONS

Eugene, Oregon

SEVEN LAST WORDS & EIGHT WORDS OF EASTER

Meditations for Your Journey to Pentecost

Awakening Vocations

1080 Patterson Street, #404 | Eugene OR 97405

marysharonmoore.com

ISBN-13: 978-1481823661 | ISBN-10: 1481823663

Cover photos and design: Dan Villani.

Manufactured in the United States of America on 30% postconsumer waste recycled material; Forest Stewardship Council (FSC)-certified.

CONTENTS

Table of Contents, continued

INTRODUCTION

Being deeply formed in the liturgical dimensions of Christian faith, I have long noticed that the church pays fervent attention to the forty days of Lent. People with incredibly busy and over-scheduled lives carve out time for the evening Lenten prayer group, or the weekly "Soup and Stations" on the Friday nights of Lent. We are good at almsgiving, fasting, and prayer.

In short, we do Lent well.

Holy Week, and especially those three holiest of days, beginning with the Thursday evening Supper of the Lord and culminating with the ringing Alleluias of Easter morning, brings people repeatedly back to church—and sometimes brings people back to *the* church, and to the discovery of a new and living faith.

But what about those eight weeks—fifty days— of Easter? That is a very long stretch, even for the most devout. Are we spiritually spent by the time we sing that last Alleluia of Easter morning?

Or do we simply get distracted, as the earth warms and those longer days give us the gardener's itch? Then there are all those distractions around the long season of graduation—from preschool to Ph.D. —along with Mother's Day, Father's Day, and booking reservations for summer vacation.

We get so easily distracted on our journey to Pentecost.

But what *about* those eight weeks of Easter? Traditionally the Jewish celebration of Pentecost, known as Shavuot, came fifty days after Passover, celebrating the spring harvest and the revelation of the Law at Mount Sinai. In Christian faith Pentecost is the celebration of the coming of the Holy Spirit, as in "a strong driving wind" and in "tongues as of fire" (Acts 2:2–3).

If Easter was Jesus' day, Pentecost surely is ours. Pentecost is rightly called "the birthday of the church." It is the whole point of the journey of Lent and the full revelation of Easter.

Indeed, the refrain of the responsorial psalm of Pentecost urges us toward real engagement in God's greater work: "Lord, send out your Spirit / and renew the face of the earth."

With Pentecost we realize (if but slowly) that *we,* now filled with the Holy Spirit, are the agents of that renewal in our place and time.

The work of "renewing the face of the earth" is our immediate and overarching concern and must shape and animate the very core of our Christian vocation and the church's mission.

In *Seven Last Words and Eight Words of Easter* I strive to shed light on this journey from Lent to Pentecost. Far from a mere reminiscence of an earlier time, this journey is here and now, a personal and collective journey into the unknown terrain of our twenty-first century.

It is a real journey, guided by the Holy Spirit, that is deeply self-involving and deeply vocational.

God's calling is particular, and it is always a calling to movement, to bold and generous action in the Holy Spirit for the good of this world which God still so loves.

I invite you to not merely read but to linger with, savor, and indeed digest the words within these pages. The important words are Jesus' words. The other words are mine, given to me, actually, to scribe as faithfully as I was able.

Some of these words will confront you with unexpected challenge. And some of these words will offer you unexpected encouragement, consolation, and joy.

All of these words serve as invitation to *you,* to enter more deeply into the mystery of the crucified and risen Lord, God's holy Fool, who taught what he knew, who stood by his words, and who could not back away from God's scandalous outpouring of friendship, kinship, and mercy.

I pray that as you ponder these *Seven Last Words and Eight Words of Easter* you will be courageous with the fire of Pentecost to *be* church, to teach what you know is true, to stand by your words, and to never back away from the scandal of God's redeeming love.

Mary Sharon Moore

February 2013

PART I

SEVEN LAST WORDS

1

THE FIRST WORD

"Father, forgive them,

they know not what they do."

Luke 23:34

No, no. This is all wrong. What my eyes now witness my heart cannot accept.

You taught a radical way of love, and like so many others, I was irresistibly drawn to you.

Your moral standard was way beyond ours. You continually challenged my view of things, especially when it came to relationships and getting my just due.

"When someone strikes you on one check," you taught, "turn and offer the other. If someone wants to sue you for what is rightfully yours, hand over the accessories as well."

But I had no idea, my Lord, how much you really meant what you said, with no exceptions.

"Love not just your neighbors," you often told us, "but your enemies. Pray for those who persecute you."

My soul is sickened to look at you now, your torn flesh fastened to this cross.

"Pray for those who persecute you," I still hear you say, your words strong and clear, as though spoken only yesterday.

I remember how you looked at me, your eyes burning those words directly into my soul.

In that moment I died a thousand deaths, knowing full well that you were challenging my pride, my self-justification, my arrogant attitude, my resistance, my need to be right.

I remember how you looked at me, your eyes burning those words directly into my soul.

Pray for those who persecute you, you insisted.

And now, my Teacher, my Lord, you utter these words: "Father, forgive them. They know not what they do."

I am filled with rage at what they have done to you, my Lord. You did no wrong. They had no right to scourge you and condemn you to death.

That crowd that called for your execution did not know you. You were nothing to them, an obstacle, an inconvenience to their way of life. I am blinded by anger. Yet even your bloodied flesh emits a strange peace.

Father, forgive them. They know not what they do.

In my brief years in your company, was this how you looked upon me and prayed for me as well? The years before we met, those years I never accounted for, and that you never asked about? Did you pray those same words to your Father—"Forgive her; she knew not what she did"?

You have covered my shame with your cloak of mercy. And now, in your last hours, as life leaks away from you, you throw that same cloak of mercy around these soldiers and executioners on whom your mercy seems wasted. But that does not stop you from speaking these words: "Father, forgive them. They know not what they do."

MEDITATION FOR THE JOURNEY ...

Linger a while with this scene and these words. Read and savor this reflection again. Then ask yourself ...

- What is new for me in this reflection? Or, what resonates within me at a deeper level?

- What moral circumstance in *my* life comes into a new or clearer light?

- What words can I bring to the Lord as I meditate on his great love?

- What is the unbidden grace for me in this reflection?

"Father, forgive them, they know not what they do."

2

THE SECOND WORD

"Today you will be with me

in Paradise."

Luke 23:43

My Lord, the process of death overcomes you as you hang upon the cross. You seem to not resist death's hideous and final grip on you.

You gave us every opportunity to understand that you are Son of God, thoroughly of God. And now, now, you are returning to your Father.

Day after day you gave us every reason to believe

that you were the Messiah, the Anointed One of God. You indulged us in unimaginable relationship with God.

By drawing us into your friendship you insisted that we, like you, address God as our Father.

That was the scandal. Not any criminal behavior on your part but your insistence that God is *our* Father—indeed, our Abba. Who was I to ever be given such a privilege?

Yet you insisted, in the name of friendship, that I share in that same intimate, trusting relationship you shared with your Father.

That was the scandal, your insistence that God is our Father—indeed, our Abba. Who was I to ever be given such a privilege?

I hear one of the crucified criminals mocking you. As his strength and breath diminish he musters up his last reserves to insult you.

Messiah, he sneers, save yourself. *Messiah,* he hisses. He has no idea what he is saying. If he knew you, he would speak that word with reverence. I want to shield you from his mocking, but it's too late. His words pierce the hot, oppressive air.

Now the other crucified criminal gasps for breath and rebukes him. Too wasted to turn his head sideways, he cries out to the horizon, "Have you no fear of God? We have been condemned justly. But this One has done no wrong."

Did he know you? Was he at the edge of the crowds that followed you? Did his sister speak of you? Was his brother one of those you healed?

This second criminal falls silent. And with excruciating pain he turns his face toward you. "Jesus," he says in a parched whisper, "remember me when you come into your kingdom."

Remember me, he says. *Remember me.* His plea hangs like thin hope suspended by a gossamer thread. *Remember me.*

He doesn't say, "Rescue me." He doesn't say, "Take me with you into your kingdom." He simply asks the small favor, *Remember me.*

This penitent thief speaks your name, my Lord. "Jesus," he addresses you. Your sacred name rests a moment on his parched and blood-caked lips, those lips a brief resting place for your name which I reverence.

Jesus, remember me.

A sigh of joy issues from your own lips. "Amen," you say to him. *May it be,* and still more, *so it is.*

You lean your sacred head toward this hopeful penitent, and you speak the most blessed words: "Today you will be with me in paradise."

Today you promise him, as the two of you go through this passage of death together, that he is not outside your love, but that he will dwell with you in the house of Love, the dwelling place of the blessed.

Now I begin to understand what you meant when you taught us, "I am the Way."

MEDITATION FOR THE JOURNEY ...

Linger a while with this scene and these words. Read and savor this reflection again. Then ask yourself ...

• What captures my imagination in this reflection? Or, what rings true in a new way?

• What circumstance of wounding or forgiveness in my life comes into a new or clearer light?

• What forgiveness do I still need to speak to someone? What forgiveness do I still need to speak to myself?

• What is the unbidden grace for me in this reflection?

"Today you will be with me in Paradise."

3

THE THIRD WORD

"Woman, behold your son. …

Behold, your mother."

John 19:26–27

This scorching afternoon wears on. I have no memory of life outside this agony. Every minute explodes and unravels like a personal eternity as you twist, my Lord, finding no relief from the weight of your body pulling against the nails that hold you to the cross.

I stand here helpless.

If I were to touch your raw, torn flesh, torture would shoot out from every exposed nerve. Crows flap and caw noisily in the distance, lured by the scent of blood and baking flesh.

I am drawn out of my personal grief by the solemn, steadfast presence of your mother.

The quiet dignity and profound serenity that has always defined her now becomes a mantle of strength for her and for the few who stand with her.

For some time now your eyes have sunken backward, your eyelids closed, your jaw hanging loose. The crown of thorns has sunk into your forehead.

But now, unexplainably, you rally, and look down into the eyes of your mother. Her body shudders as her soul howls its unspeakable anguish.

Waves of her grief crash

But now,
unexplainably,
you rally,
and look down
into the eyes
of your mother.
Her body shudders
as her soul
howls its
unspeakable
anguish.

over and through the other women, and crash over me.

The disciple whom you loved comforts your mother, two souls silently howling together a grief beyond imagining.

Your heart undergoes its own inner crucifixion, incapable as you are of holding your mother in your arms to comfort her.

Of all of us who sat in your presence to receive your teaching, it was the beloved disciple who seemed in a quiet way to dwell in the heart of your words.

Especially last night at table, when you prayed that prayer of most intimate indwelling—you abiding in your Father, we abiding in you, you abiding in us— your beloved disciple received these words as balm and consolation and utter truth.

And now, I too begin to understand the divine gift of this holy abiding. Your beloved disciple looks up to meet your gaze.

Forgive me, my Lord, but I sense your heart has become a flame—no, a raging fire of love and of sorrow.

You writhe your body upward for a sharp-pained gasp of air, and you say to your mother, "Woman, behold, your son." And in utter selfless surrender you say to your beloved disciple, "Behold, your mother."

In those brief years with you, could this young, cherished disciple ever imagine the role he would be given in your absence? Could he ever imagine a time when you would be gone?

Yet with great love you have formed him, guided him, set him apart for this special portion of favor and grace.

You have rendered him worthy to stand in your place as caregiver and comfort for your revered and grieving mother.

This moment is too private, too privileged. I feel awkward in this intimate moment of your leave-taking from your mother.

No one moves. Everyone understands. You really are leaving us. Death overshadows you. With grace you submit.

MEDITATION FOR THE JOURNEY …

Linger a while with this scene and these words. Read and savor this reflection again. Then ask yourself …

• What phrase or image speaks to me in this reflection? Or, what resonates at a deeper level?

• What friend or loved one have I had to release to the hard work of dying? What has that letting go been like for me?

• What is the unbidden grace for me in this reflection?

"Woman, behold your son. … Behold, your mother."

4

THE FOURTH WORD

"My God, my God,

why have you forsaken me?"

Mark 15:34

My Lord, you have hung upon this cross for nearly three hours now, writhing under a blazing sun and sinking into a slow and hideous death.

You have done nothing, nothing, to deserve this punishment—the mock trial, the scourging, this crown of thorns.

And now, a slow and public death by crucifixion.

You have been stripped of every human dignity, your flesh now exposed like the raw flesh of some slain animal left for birds of prey.

Suddenly a strange darkness has come over the land. Even earth and sky know that something is terribly wrong. Fastened as you are to the cross, you are powerless to release yourself from this torture. And I am powerless to ease your pain.

We seem suspended in time, caught on the precipice of eternity, waiting on God who seems to have left you on your own.

How could the heart of your Father not be moved?

People pass by on this road into the city, jeering at you, crucified as you are with common criminals, on public display as life bleeds out of you.

We seem suspended in time, caught on the precipice of eternity, waiting on God who seems to have left you on your own. How could the heart of your Father not be moved?

The sign above your head reads: "King of the Jews." People point and laugh as they walk by.

They know you well enough. "He saved others," they jeer, "yet he cannot save himself."

Yet I know you. You are the Beloved of your Father. You never claimed privilege. You claimed only your Father's abiding love.

I recall your nights of solitude, after a day of people hemming you in on every side, and you freeing them from illness, unshackling them from sin. As night pressed on toward dawn you could be found in the empty spaces outside of town, deep in prayer with your Father.

You taught us your prayer language, the psalms. When you prayed, those psalms came alive with meaning, revealing to us an absolute trust in God.

That utter abandonment to your Father's willing shaped every aspect of your life, your mission, your teaching, your healing. When you prayed the psalms, you led us to our own deepest truth, that God alone is the faithful One.

And now you stir, agitated and straining for breath. In a broken voice you cry out, "My God, my God, why have you forsaken me?"

Instantly I recognize this line from a psalm that you often prayed for a world too broken to pray on its own. I recall how that psalm continues:

"Why are you so far from helping me, / from the words of my groaning? / O my God, I cry by day, but you do not answer; / and by night, but I find no rest. / Yet you are holy."

By your own unshakable trust in your Father you taught us to fiercely cling to that trust at all times, for God is worthy. You taught us that lesson, my Lord.

We both know every line of that psalm and how it ends. *I may enter into the grip of a hideous death,* the Psalmist prays, *yet you, O God, are God, and you are worthy.*

MEDITATION FOR THE JOURNEY ...

Linger a while with this scene and these words. Read and savor this reflection again. Then ask yourself ...

• What unexpected insight does this reflection offer me concerning prayer?

• Is my prayer strong and true enough to sustain me in my hour of anguish?

• How might the Lord be inviting me into deeper relationship with him through the Psalms?

• What is the unbidden grace for me in this reflection?

"My God, my God, why have you forsaken me?"

5

THE FIFTH WORD

"I thirst."

John 19:28

"I thirst," you say at last.

My Lord, with excruciating pain you heave your body upward and gasp for breath as the force of life escapes you. The scorching sun sears your torn and bloodied flesh.

And now you, the Lord of Life, speak these humble words: *I thirst.*

How often we prayed together the words of the

Psalmist: "Like dry broken clay is my throat, / my tongue sticks to my palate, / you lay me in the dust of death."

Yet I am startled, shaken and terrified to the core of my being, to see you, my Lord, so bereft of life. I stand in shame, convicted in my self-seeking as I behold the utter poverty from which you speak these simple words: *I thirst.*

Marred beyond recognition is the lovely One I knew, who promised springs of living water. You were full of grace; you were God's Beloved.

Your goodness was more than this world deserved, more than I have ever deserved.

Yet this world is where you chose to dwell. It is our wounds you chose to touch, our infirmities which you chose to heal.

Your absolute poverty takes me to the bitter dregs of the poverties I try so hard to hide.

Your plea rings in my ears: *I thirst.* Your helplessness crashes through me. Your absolute poverty takes me to the bitter dregs of the poverties I try so hard to hide.

Your utter abandonment to your Father's plan smashes every illusion I have ever had of greatness and capability and success. I have carefully cultivated my life, while you have freely thrown yours into the mystery of your Father's plan.

Why don't I just walk away now?

"I thirst," you say. It's true: I cannot leave you, yet I cannot relieve you of your poverty before God and before the world. I cannot snatch you from the jaws of this hideous and unjust death.

Like you, I am powerless before the inescapable ways of your Father's willing.

"I thirst," I, too, whisper now. These humbling words echo with a thunderous roar in my soul. These are the true words, which, if I were honest, I would have cried out long ago.

I thirst. Truth be told, I am delirious with thirst for God, just as you were, my Lord, all along.

These were the words of the Psalmist that we

prayed together so often: "As the deer longs for running streams, / so my soul longs for you, my God. / My whole being thirsts for God, my living God. / When can I go and see the face of God?"

I thirst. Your words, my Lord, plunge me into the depths of my radical need for God, in whom alone my soul, with yours, can be at rest.

MEDITATION FOR THE JOURNEY ...

Linger a while with this scene and these words. Read and savor this reflection again. Then ask yourself ...

• What new insight does this reflection offer me? Or, what resonates within me at a deeper level?

• What interior thirst of my own becomes more apparent to me?

• How is the Lord inviting me into more intimate, more responsible relationship with him?

• What is the unbidden grace for me in this reflection?

"I thirst."

6

THE SIXTH WORD

"It is finished."

John 19:30

The sun blasts forth its furnace heat. For as far as my eye can see, the landscape blanches in the relentless blaze. Waves of radiant heat force everything before me into a mirage-like dance.

No one can escape this fiery heat, my Lord, especially you, as your raw flesh slowly roasts.

You hang between life and death, between heaven and this blood-soaked earth.

A surprising chill rushes across my face, an unexplainable chill sending a shiver through my body.

In extreme anguish, you push yourself upward for one last tortuous breath. In words which only you can truly understand, you say simply: "It is finished."

In words which only you can truly understand, you say simply: "It is finished."

Slowly, and with great anguish, you turn your head. Your ribs barely move as you draw the most fragile breath.

A thunderous silence overtakes me as my world, with yours, is hurled into the abyss.

Today, it seems, not even God has a word to speak. *It is finished.*

"God's hopeful work of mercy has failed," the moment seems to say. You die, my Lord, not surrounded by the symbols of success but rather, pierced by the symbols of humiliating failure.

It is finished. Your words hang in the still, stifling air.

Your words reverberate off the far distant walls of the universe and come crashing back to the core of my soul. *It is finished.*

No more cherished encounters with you, no more consolation of friendship with the only One who ever truly knew my soul.

It is finished, you say, and now I understand that you are referring not to your mortal life but to your selfless mission, the fulfillment of your Father's willing.

I remember your words when you told us that we are in you and of you like branches of the vine. "I came so that you might have life," you said, "and have it abundantly."

This was your mission, you taught us, that by your living and your dying we might become unshackled, forgiven, and set free for God's abundant life. We didn't get it.

This is what is finished—your payment of the price for our redemption, restoring us to right relationship with God and with one another.

You speak the most anguished words, my Lord, and the sweetest words. This completion of your mission is the moment when I am restored to friendship with our God.

This is your hour, of which you often spoke, your hour of fulfillment through humble obedience to your Father's deepest desire—that we dwell in you as you, my Lord, dwell in him.

MEDITATION FOR THE JOURNEY …

Linger a while with this scene and these words. Read and savor this reflection again. Then ask yourself …

• What phrase or image is new for me in this reflection?

• Will my mission be clear enough to allow me to say, with Jesus, *"It is finished"*? What is that mission?

• Through his example, how is the Lord inviting me into deeper relationship with him?

• What is the unbidden grace for me in this reflection?

"It is finished."

7

THE SEVENTH WORD

"Father, into your hands I commend

my spirit."

Luke 23:46

A strange darkness rushes down from the hill of the city, a giant wave of chilling darkness rushes toward the mob and overtakes the place where three men hang in crucifixion.

The scorching temperature suddenly drops as the moon eclipses the sun. The soul shudders, as though awakening alone in an alien land.

Word runs with alarming speed through the crowd that the veil of the temple has been torn in two.

I want to run, but to where? I want to hide, but no shelter can offer me the consolation I seek.

The women who have stood with you through this ordeal, my Lord, remain with you now. The beloved disciple, too, stands helpless but steadfast nonetheless, as you undergo the sentence of an unjust and violent death.

Now a silence comes over the mob. The air seems to crackle with eerie anticipation. Crows that had been cawing and circling for hours now have disappeared.

The weight of this stillness is almost too much to bear. How long, O Lord?

You have not stirred for several minutes.

Just when I think surely that death has come, I see a twitch of raw muscle, a near imperceptible movement of your eyelids, the slow, unsteady movement of your chest as you strain for what little breath you can snatch.

And now I see you push yourself up for one last agonized gasp of air, and you cry out from the depths of your soul, "Father."

The word pierces the air. I feel like an intruder as you address, one final time, the One who has been your life, your food.

Your cry pierces the heavens and falls back to earth like fine ash. We wait, because you are not yet finished speaking.

Your eyes gaze heavenward. You no longer see us, but see now what we cannot see.

You speak as though you have passed through the anguish, your voice now surprisingly at peace even as you struggle to form and speak the words.

"Father, into your hands

You speak
as though you
have passed through
the anguish,
your voice
now surprisingly
at peace
even as you
struggle to form
and speak
the words.

I commend my spirit." And now, having said this, my Lord, you breathe your last breath.

That's all. A life is finished.

Not just any life, but the life of the One in whom we had hoped, the One who did no wrong, the One who did not deserve to be condemned to death.

No one moves. For those who loved you, we never imagined ourselves without you. You were the center of our lives, and now a hollow vacancy invades us to the core.

Your work is completed. You are at peace.

As for us, in this moment, we are lost, spiritually paralyzed by shock and grief.

But we are, at least. together.

MEDITATION FOR THE JOURNEY ...

Linger a while with this scene and these words. Read and savor this reflection again. Then ask yourself ...

• What sobering or hopeful truth does this reflection offer to me?

• What might be *my* final words? What will I most want to express with my final breath?

• In this reflection, how is the Lord inviting me into more responsible relationship with him?

• What is the unbidden grace for me in this reflection?

"Father, into your hands I commend my spirit."

PART II

EIGHT WORDS
OF EASTER

8

THE FIRST WORD OF EASTER

"Woman, why are you weeping?"

John 20:15

We walk about the house like dead people. No one speaks. No one can think of anything to say, nor even find the energy to imagine conversation.

Overcome with grief, we cannot picture any real future for our lives. All meaning is gone.

Our one consolation is the rhythm of the days. Sabbath is now over.

Before the break of dawn on the first day of the

week, one of our group, Mary of Magdala, stirs from sleep and goes out into the street, out to the edge of town, to the burial site.

When she arrives at your tomb, my Lord, something isn't right. She wonders: *Is this a troubled dream? The stone is rolled away.*

A shiver of fear runs through her. "The body of my Lord has been taken away," she thinks, and runs back to the house to alert the others.

Now Peter and the beloved disciple run with Mary to the tomb, and see things just as she described them.

But Mary stays outside the tomb weeping, as though someone has pulled the scab off the wound of her grief.

They peer into the tomb, and they too find it empty. What should they make of this? Confused and shaken, they too return to the house.

But Mary stays outside the tomb weeping, as though someone has pulled the scab off the wound of her grief.

Unthinking, or perhaps out of sheer hope, she peers one more time into the tomb.

Two angels seated there ask her: "Woman, why are you weeping?"

A nonsense question, she thinks; how can I not weep? The center of my life has been ripped away from me.

And why, she does not know, but as though some magnetic presence were at her back, she turns around.

A man is standing there. The gardener? She hadn't heard him approach.

"Woman," the man asks, "why are you weeping?"

The words run through her like a shock of cold water. "Why does this man's question flood my soul with hope?" she wonders.

His gaze is steady, penetrating, and full of love. "Whom are you looking for?" he asks.

His voice carries a tone of authority and quiet dignity.

That question, she thinks, wasn't that the question Jesus asked of those who came to arrest him in the garden?

Whom are you looking for?

This man seems too knowing. The answer is obvious. The stone is unexplainably rolled away, the tomb unsealed and empty. The body of Jesus is missing.

"Sir, if you carried him away, tell me where you laid him, and I will take him."

Clearly she does not know what she is saying. Delirious with grief, she simply wants the body of her beloved Lord given its due dignity and proper burial.

The man's gaze remains steady, penetrating, full of love. He does not share her grief, yet he seems no stranger to her soul.

"Mary!" he says to her.

Everything she knows and understands suddenly shifts. "Rabbouni," she says to him.

She stands, yes, before her living Lord, yet

everything has changed. It is the same Lord, but the relationship is new.

MEDITATION FOR THE JOURNEY ...

Linger a while with this scene and these words. Read and savor this reflection again. Then ask yourself ...

- What words or images seem new to me in this reflection? Or, what resonates at a deeper level?

- What irreversible loss have I grieved in my life? What loss have I not yet grieved?

- How is the Lord inviting me into more trusting relationship with him through my loss?

- What is the unbidden grace for me in this reflection?

"Woman, why are you weeping?"

9

THE SECOND WORD OF EASTER

"Go tell my brothers."

Matthew 28:10

This new reality is altogether too much for us. The stories run together, details become confused. We each speak what we can recall, drawing on memories shaped by grief and incomprehension.

Some of the women recall how they headed out at dawn following the close of Sabbath, and went to see the tomb.

There's something about an earthquake, an angel

—two angels? No, only one, descending like a lightning bolt from heaven. And rolling back the stone that sealed the tomb, the angel sits upon it.

The guards assigned to the tomb, overcome by this angel's presence, lay like dead men.

Dreamlike we hear the angel speak words of holy nonsense. "Do not be afraid!" the angel says. *Do not be afraid.*

Wasn't that the exact phrase Jesus often spoke when things seemed most hopeless?

These words spoken now reassure us enough to at least understand that this is God's messenger, with indeed a message of holy nonsense.

"You are seeking Jesus the crucified. He is not here."

At this point all we know is Jesus the crucified, the One who died and was buried here.

The events of three days ago are a burning wound in our memory. Yet what does this divine messenger say? "Go quickly and tell his disciples, 'He has been raised.'"

We run from the tomb toward the house where the disciples are staying.

Do not be afraid, we recall the angel saying. *He has been raised; go tell his disciples.*

[W]e run as though we are racing against time, racing ahead of some giant wave of fear.

We turn these phrases over and over in our hearts, committing them to memory.

Trying to outpace each other and near breathless, we run as though we are racing against time, racing ahead of some giant wave of fear.

And suddenly before us is Jesus, standing in the road as though to interrupt our run. We collapse at his feet, completely astonished.

Truly, this is holy nonsense. We are overcome with joy and an outpouring of worship we have never known before.

And Jesus says to us: "Do not be afraid. Go tell my brothers to go to Galilee, and there they will see me."

Back at the tomb, in our grief, we were not just imagining that angel. Jesus' words to us confirm the message.

As the events of the morning settle, we reflect on what is happening—Jesus, risen from the dead, a new reality that changes everything, *everything*.

The empty tomb now seems like a shell, like old skin, like an abandoned chrysalis.

What comes next we do not know. But we are to tell the brothers: "Go to Galilee where you will find the risen Lord."

MEDITATION FOR THE JOURNEY ...

Linger a while with this scene and these words. Read and savor this reflection again. Then ask yourself ...

• What new insight comes forward for me in this reflection? Or, what resonates at a deeper level?

• In what troubled situation in my life have I been astonished to suddenly encounter the Lord?

• What word might the Lord wish to speak to me now in the circumstances of my life?

• What is the unbidden grace for me in this reflection?

"Go tell my brothers."

10

THE THIRD WORD OF EASTER

"Stop holding on to me."

John 20:17

Only some days later, when the house had quieted down, did Mary of Magdala openly reflect on the words the risen Lord spoke to her on that first morning.

Indeed, all of her experience since then seems to be shaped by the events of that morning when everything changed, the morning of Jesus' resurrection.

"He spoke my name," she recalls as we sit by the window. "And when he spoke it, I felt as though my entire life was called into being. I felt that now I was fully myself, when the risen Lord spoke my name."

Her voice trails off, and she looks out the window into the distance.

We sit in the silence for a while, letting memories of that first morning come forward, refracted like fleeting shards of light dancing through a prism. Mary picks up the conversation.

"After he spoke my name he said something to me that wounded me. I tried to not show the hurt and the shock I felt at his words, but I know that he understood what I was feeling."

Mary of Magdala turns to face me directly.

"He said to me, 'Stop holding on to me.' Those words burned through me. The Teacher had never spoken to me that way. I felt as though I were holding him down."

She pauses.

Mary of Magdala turns to face me directly.

"He said to me, 'Stop holding on to me.' … The Teacher had never spoken to me that way."

"Indeed, his words to me were: 'Stop holding on to me, for I have not yet ascended to the Father.'"

Finally I could name in my own understanding what the Magdalene had also come to know: Jesus has experienced something that we have not.

He knows fully what we glimpse only dimly.

Indeed he has gone before us, not only into Galilee but into a fullness of life in communion with his Father that we can only imagine, the fullness of that divine communion that he promised us on the night of his arrest.

Stop holding on to me, he had said.

Let go of what you knew of me when I was still with you. What you have heard, what you have seen with your eyes, what you have looked upon and touched with your hands—all of this was my teaching you about the Father. Now, I go before you.

Now, he said, *I return to my Father and your Father, to my God and your God.* I will no longer teach you. Rather, I will breathe on you the Holy Spirit who will guide you in all things.

Mary of Magdala pauses, sits back in her chair.

I can see that these past few days have changed her. Beyond the exhaustion she seems to possess a spiritual insight that will hold us all together.

"All I know," she says to me, "is that we are the Lord's. He promised us that he would not abandon us. We are his now. What we shall become, and what will become of our lives, has not yet been revealed."

MEDITATION FOR THE JOURNEY ...

Linger a while with this scene and these words. Read and savor this reflection again. Then ask yourself ...

• What words or images speak to me in this reflection?

• In what ways does my own life in relation to the risen Lord come into a new or clearer light?

• How is the Lord inviting me into more intimate, more responsible relationship with him?

• What is the unbidden grace for me in this reflection?

"Stop holding on to me."

11

THE FOURTH WORD OF EASTER

"What are you discussing

as you walk along?"

Luke 24:17

This first week has been a blur for the band of us who had followed Jesus. Ten of the Eleven quickly got word of his resurrection, and the women were there at dawn, at the start of it all.

But many disciples outside the core group did not get the news of Jesus' resurrection right away.

Two of them later recalled how, with all the

political turmoil around Jesus' death, and the danger of being identified as his followers, they decided to head out of Jerusalem on the road to Emmaus, a town whose location I don't really know.

In fact, people I've talked to don't seem to know this town. It seems that these disciples were on the road to nowhere.

The way they were feeling, they said, it certainly felt that way.

"We believe that this was the Messiah who was crucified," one of them told me. "But my traveling companion and I argued over how, if Jesus was the Messiah, he could be condemned to death and actually crucified. What happened to him didn't fit the script."

I wanted to tell him that the script no longer applied. But I didn't need to tell him anything. He had more story to share.

It seems that these disciples were on the road to nowhere.

The way they were feeling, they said, it certainly felt that way.

"As we were walking," the disciple continued, "another traveler approached us. He could see that we were pretty deep in debate, so he asked us, 'What are you discussing as you walk along?'

"My traveling partner Cleopas answered, 'Are you the only visitor to Jerusalem who does not know of the things that have taken place there in these days?'"

While this disciple recalled his story I sensed already one more instance of that now familiar pattern of not knowing and knowing, not seeing and seeing, the appearing and the vanishing that defined these early appearances of the risen Lord.

"What did the stranger say?" I asked, listening closely to the disciples' choice of words.

"The stranger replied, 'What sort of things?'" the disciples recounted. "He never did answer Yes or No as to whether he knew what was going on. He seemed interested in our take on what had happened concerning Jesus. So we told him.

"Then this man took us to task for being so slow of heart to believe all that the prophets spoke. And in a few brilliant brush strokes he painted all that referred to the Messiah in the scriptures.

"That night when we stopped to share a meal, our eyes were opened and in the breaking of the bread we recognized the risen Lord. Then we understood—*then we understood*—why our hearts were burning within us while he spoke to us on the way."

This disciple gave words to what I too have been feeling these past few days. And I now recognize a new quality of our discipleship: Our hearts now burn within us.

MEDITATION FOR THE JOURNEY ...

Linger a while with this scene and these words. Read and savor this reflection again. Then ask yourself ...

• What phrase or image in this reflection offers me new insight?

• When have my eyes and my understanding been unexpectedly opened to the Lord's presence?

• How is the Lord inviting me at this point in my life into a deeper experience of discipleship?

• What is the unbidden grace for me in this reflection?

"What are you discussing as you walk along?"

12

THE FIFTH WORD OF EASTER

"Peace be with you."

Luke 24:36

My Lord, my heart is in a tailspin. I don't recall when I last had a full night of sleep. A week ago? Maybe longer?

Your arrest seems like a distant memory. The mock trial and your crucifixion seem like some fading troubled dream.

And now everything is changed. We want to get our arms around what is happening. We want to be with you again, just to sit in your presence, and to learn from you our Teacher what you have experienced.

But you seem to escape us, here and then vanished, suddenly appearing and then just as suddenly you are gone.

Yes, our hearts do burn within us, because our hearts know something that our minds cannot grasp.

We are made for something far more than we can now imagine. Your resurrection points to our own destiny.

We are made for something far more than we can now imagine. Your resurrection points to our own destiny.

And now these two disciples have returned to Jerusalem to tell us of their encounter with you on the road and in the breaking of the bread.

As we gather in the upper room our hearts are full of amazement and expectation. Our words tumble out over themselves to express what we have witnessed in these recent days.

In fact, anything we say seems to fall short of the reality we have encountered. The air seems filled with sparks of light and hope, and inwardly we shake with awe and wonder.

And suddenly, you appear again, as though these crackling sparks of light have coalesced into the very flesh of God. The room stills.

As though struck by lightning we become incapable of speech. I feel as though the walls of my soul have vanished, unleashing an infinite capacity within me for the light of your glory.

With a smile filled with mystery and love, you extend your arms, your hands, and say slowly with blazing intention, "Peace be with you."

For a long moment we are stunned. We are filled with a new peace which immediately finds a home in us, a peace which clearly flows straight from your resurrection.

How much time elapses, I don't know. You have caught us by surprise. Snatching us from fear, you have caught us up into the inner courts of heaven.

In the unexpected moment we are not ourselves, or maybe we are beyond ourselves.

Yet strangely I feel more truly myself than I could ever imagine.

The room is silent. Your words reverberate in the stillness as we take this moment to heart.

And now, my Lord, you gently chide us: "Why are you terrified?" you ask. "Look at my hands, my feet. Touch me and see—a ghost does not have flesh and bones as I have."

You, too, seem filled with an incredulous joy. You bring us back to our senses with a simple question: "Have you anything here to eat?"

Quickly from the hearth we bring you a piece of baked fish, and you take it and eat it.

You savor it. You smile.

A holy laughter breaks out and fills the room. Our eyes are filled, too, with tears of sheer joy, a joy that breaks through our exhaustion.

I feel sealed, my Lord, in your holy gift of peace. In this moment I know with certainty that no one, no trial, no adversity can ever take your gift of peace away from me.

MEDITATION FOR THE JOURNEY ...

Linger a while with this scene and these words. Read and savor this reflection again. Then ask yourself ...

• What do I experience in this reflection? Or, what resonates within me at a deeper level?

• In my life, what situation that holds me in the grip of fear might be shifting now?

• In what specific way is the Lord inviting me into more trusting relationship with him?

• What is the unbidden grace for me in this reflection?

"Peace be with you."

13

THE SIXTH WORD OF EASTER

"As the Father has sent me,

so I send you."

John 20:21

Ever the most excellent Teacher, you, my Lord, know when your words have not yet reached their deepest level within your disciples.

You never explain your teaching. You do not waste words. You simply repeat what we need to hear, and receive, and take to heart.

As we stand in your presence and you stand in

our midst, you say to us again, "Peace be with you."

Unrushed, you search from face to face, pouring from your eyes into the eyes of each of us, one by one, the peace which is your gift, the distinctive gift of your resurrection.

You pour into us your peace, as though it were liquid gold, pouring until you see that we are truly filled, thoroughly filled, with your gift of resurrection peace.

You pour into us your peace, as though it were liquid gold, pouring until you see that we are truly filled, thoroughly filled, with your gift of resurrection peace.

And now in a solemn tone you say to us, "As the Father has sent me, so I send you."

How shall I put into words what I experience in this moment? I feel completely washed of the weariness of my grieving.

As I stand among my fellow disciples I feel thoroughly known, valued for who I am in your eyes.

I feel as though you have just gifted me, ever so lovingly, with the gift of my own holy personhood.

Each of us and soon all of us together sense the divine communion of this moment. We now realize that we no longer are mere disciples, learners planted at the feet of the Teacher.

No, now we have become a community of love, your beloved community, bound together in your gift of peace.

As the Father has sent me, you say, *so I send you.*

In silence we thoughtfully chew on these words, spoken by our Teacher, spoken by our crucified and risen Lord.

We chew on them as though chewing on the bread which you blessed, broke, and shared with us.

And in the silence something slowly awakens within us.

I begin to realize: These years of sitting at the feet of my Lord weren't just about learning about his Father, or about the ways of the reign of God.

These years of learning were my apprenticeship. Your teachings had a point.

As you have lived, so I now must live. As you have done, so I now must do.

Yes, the weariness *is* washed away. I feel thoroughly and undeniably known and valued in the eyes of my risen Lord.

Yes, I feel deeply secure in his resurrection peace. And what I begin to glimpse in this moment is the sobering implication of giving myself to this One who is my Truth.

My life now becomes woven into the divine and perfect weave. *As the Father has sent me, so I send you.*

Indeed, these years of apprenticeship were preparing me for this very moment. Why did I not see it? But then, how could I?

Sent to do what? I wonder. To teach? to preach? to heal? To live this Truth which I carry in my flesh and bones?

To witness unflinchingly before those who have

the power and a presumed right to destroy me? Sent to do what?

To pour out my life in self-offering, lovingly for the sake of the world, as my crucified and risen Lord has done?

Where are the boundaries of self-offering to the Lord?

I begin to sense: *There are none.*

In this moment I have more questions than answers. More questions, that is, until they fade away.

The only certainty for me now is this peace which permeates every fiber of my being.

MEDITATION FOR THE JOURNEY ...

Linger a while with this scene and these words. Read and savor this reflection again. Then ask yourself ...

• What truth, what new understanding, comes forward for me in this reflection?

• What boundaries do I easily set around my self-offering to the Lord? What courageous step must I take to move beyond these boundaries?

• How is the Lord inviting me into more intimate, more responsible relationship with him?

• What is the unbidden grace for me in this reflection?

"As the Father has sent me, so I send you."

14

THE SEVENTH WORD OF EASTER

"Receive the holy Spirit."

John 20:22

I am lost in my thoughts, my Lord, standing in your presence among fellow disciples who seem lost in their thoughts, too.

Since you entered into our midst moments ago, you are the one who has done the talking, and your words, though few, have filled this room with an enormous spirit.

Our initial joy at seeing you has become

contoured by a more sobering awareness.

As the silence now settles more deeply, we slowly awaken more fully to the truth: God has invested everything in us. In our redemption, yes. But even more.

For all those whose lives you touched, my Lord, we somehow were the odd band you drew together to learn from you directly.

You held back nothing in what you taught, in what you revealed, although much of what you shared was lost on us.

My mind begins to reel. Your words, just spoken, seem eternally emblazoned on my soul.

As your Father has sent you, so now you send us.

I feel faint, and wonder if anyone else in this room feels the way I do.

The room is filled with a stunned silence. I glance around at my fellow disciples. Their eyes seem lost in an inward, eternal gaze, their faces fixed in gentle mystery as the Master's words find a place to lodge within them.

I glance around
at my fellow disciples.
Their eyes seem
lost in an inward,
eternal gaze,
their faces
fixed in
gentle mystery
as the Master's
words find
a place to lodge
within them.

And now you extend your arms and stretch your nail-scarred and radiant hands outward over us.

With eyes shut you inhale deeply, and then slowly exhale—once, twice, three times—and you say, "Receive the holy Spirit."

I recall your last deeply labored breaths as you hung upon the cross, and how you cried out to your Father, "Receive my spirit."

And the breath left you. Here you are now, breathing new life, new spirit, the promised Holy Spirit, into us.

This moment of complete and lavish anointing is too much for me, too large, too real.

And yet I sense the utter perfection and grace of this moment, of my being here, of our being here, all of us together.

Hungrily I breathe in the Spirit of my risen Lord. The room is filled with the sounds of others hungrily breathing in the Spirit.

In my mind's eye I see the dry bones over which Ezekiel prophesied, "See! I will bring spirit into you, that you may come to life, make sinew and flesh and skin cover you, so that you may come to life and know that I am the Lord."

I am filled now with a new and vibrant knowing. I am awakening to an unexpected invitation—to new life in my risen Lord the Christ.

MEDITATION FOR THE JOURNEY …

Linger a while with this scene and these words. Read and savor this reflection again. Then ask yourself …

• What words or images stand out for me in this reflection? Or, what resonates within me at a deeper level?

• When did I last breathe in, deeply and intentionally, the holy Spirit of the risen Lord? Do I have the courage to do it now?

• What is the unbidden grace for me in this reflection?

"Receive the holy Spirit."

15

THE EIGHTH WORD OF EASTER

"Go, therefore, and make disciples."

Matthew 28:19

We stand before you, my Lord, no longer a disparate group of followers but now your beloved community, breathing the one breath of your holy Spirit.

We seem one flesh, one body, one Spirit in you.

We seem, in this moment, suspended between heaven and earth, clothed in a new and perfect body, a body we cannot yet fully grow into.

What we experience is a new kind of "new." I

have no words, really, to describe this encounter with you, my risen Lord.

We seem, in this moment, suspended between heaven and earth, clothed in a new and perfect body, a body we cannot yet fully grow into. What we experience is a new kind of "new."

You have breathed your holy Spirit into us, and in the ensuing silence we slowly, reverently, regulate our breathing of this new breath.

I am not asleep but awake. I know that I live, yes, but now I know it is no longer I who live but you, my risen Lord Christ, who live in me.

What I experience is nothing less than a union of breath, and spirit, and destiny, an experience of one being in God—my being, yes, yet truly and most fully yours.

When you know that we are ready to hear, you speak again: "Go, therefore," you say, "and make disciples of all nations."

I think back to that day long ago that seemed like the real beginning of my life, that day when, beckoned by your gaze, I moved from the far edge of the crowd to the center, then closer, until I found you making a place for me in the circle of those few who were sitting close to you.

You were making disciples that day, drawing to yourself those who were ready to hear your words and not back away.

You took us under your care, taught us to walk with you, to work with you, to learn the innerness of things as they work in the reign of God.

And now you tell us: Go, do as I have done. Make disciples, the next generation of disciples, and the next. Perpetuate my work.

I am filled with amazement at what you have entrusted to me, to us. You have anointed us, each one of us, in your particular and loving way, in your Spirit.

You have anointed *us* to stand in your place and to carry on your work.

A stunned silence fills the room as the enormity of our mission slowly sinks in.

"And behold," you say at last, "I am with you always, until the end of the age."

We are losing you, my Lord, yet deep down I know, not really. We will be on our own in this new mission, yet not really.

In my heart's memory I hold and cherish your words and ponder them, trying to knit them together into the new fabric of my life.

Receive my peace, you said; *be of peace, be my peace to others. For as my Father has sent me, so I send you.* These are your words.

And you have told us more: I seal you and strengthen you in my holy Spirit because my work is now your work, to make disciples of all people, all nations.

As I drew you, you say, into God's reign, so welcome others into God's reign. Do not spare the truths I have shared with you but share them fully, caringly, freely. I am with you. Now, *go.*

Meditation for the Journey …

Linger a while with this scene and these words. Read and savor this reflection again. Then ask yourself …

• What is new or even startling for me in this reflection?

• What does my discipleship look like? Not as I wish it were, but as it actually is?

• In what ways am I an actual apostle, one sent in the power of the Holy Spirit?

• What is the unbidden grace for me in this reflection?

"Go, therefore, and make disciples."

WORDS QUOTED

Matthew

28:10, 19

Mark

15:34

Luke

23:34, 43, 46; **24:**17, 36

John

19:26–27, 28, 30; **20:**15, 17, 21, 22

ABOUT THE AUTHOR

Mary Sharon Moore is a Catholic writer, speaker, and spiritual director. Her work is known for its ability to awaken and clarify the inner life in service to the church's mission—to remain in Christ, and to reveal him everywhere.

OTHER BOOKS BY MARY SHARON MOORE

and available at marysharonmoore.com:

- *Anointed for a Purpose: Confirmed for Life in the 21st Century* (2012)

- *Conformed to Christ: Discoveries in the Maturing Christ-centered Life* (2016)

- *Dare to Believe, Rise Up to Act: Equipping Laity to be the Public Face of Christ* (2019)

- *Lord, Teach Us to Pray: An Intimate Look into a Maturing Prayer Life* (2017)

- *Moving in God's Direction: Essentials of Christ-centered Spiritual and Vocational Direction* (2012)

For a free catalog of parish resources, including Dare to Believe, Rise Up to Act, to inquire about spiritual and vocational direction, or to schedule Mary Sharon Moore for a speaking date, please visit marysharonmoore.com.

Made in the USA
Las Vegas, NV
27 March 2022